Pebble® Plus

Hands-On Science Fun

How to Make a WIND SPEED METER

A 4D Book

by Barbara Alpert

PEBBLE
a capstone imprint

Pebble Plus is published by Capstone Press,
1710 Roe Crest Drive, North Mankato, Minnesota 56003
www.mycapstone.com

Library of Congress Cataloging-in-Publication Data
is available on the Library of Congress website.

ISBN 978-1-9771-0227-0 (library binding)
ISBN 978-1-9771-0518-9 (paperback)
ISBN 978-1-9771-0231-7 (ebook pdf)

Editorial Credits
Carrie Braulick Sheely, editor; Sarah Bennett, designer;
Marcy Morin, scheduler and project producer;
Sarah Schuette, photo stylist and project producer;
Katy LaVigne, production specialist

Photo Credits
All photographs by Capstone Studio/Karon Dubke except for:
Shutterstock: Claudia Harms-Warlies, 18, EgudinKa, cover
(background)

Note to Parents and Teachers

The Hands-On Science Fun set supports national science
standards related to physical science. This book describes and
illustrates making a wind speed meter. The images support
early readers in understanding the text. The repetition of words
and phrases helps early readers learn new words. This book
also introduces early readers to subject-specific vocabulary
words, which are defined in the Glossary section. Early readers
may need assistance to read some words and to use the Table of
Contents, Glossary, Read More, Internet Sites, Critical Thinking
Questions, and Index sections of the book.

1 Ask an adult to download the app.  Capstone 4D
Education

2 Scan the pages with the star.

3 Enjoy your cool stuff!

———— OR ————

Use this password at capstone4D.com

windspeed02270

Printed and bound in China.
970

Table of Contents

Safety Note:
Please ask an adult for help when
making your wind speed meter.

Getting Started

Weather always changes. How can we know what weather is coming? We can study weather patterns.

Make a wind speed meter. Use it to measure how fast the wind is blowing.

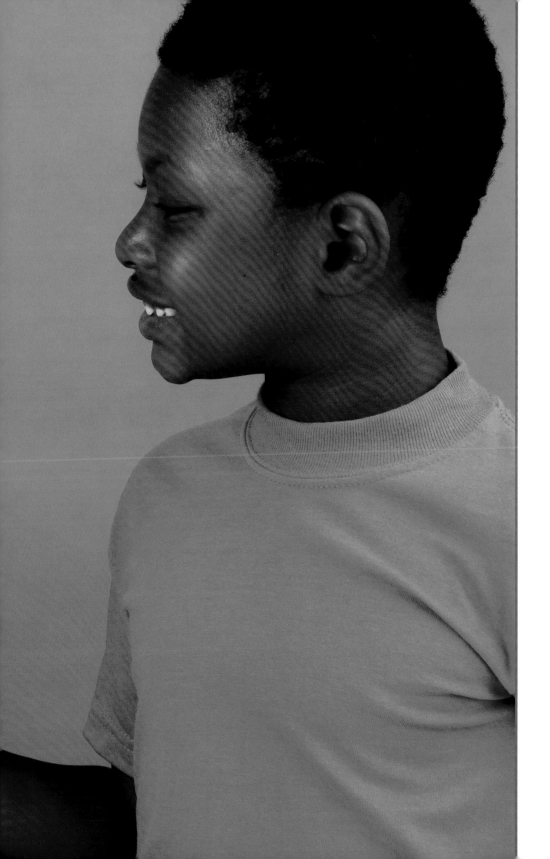

Here's what you need:

5 small paper cups

hole punch

2 plastic straws

pencil

pushpin

marker

piece of modeling clay

fan with 3 speeds

a timer that counts seconds

paper

5

Making a Wind Speed Meter

Punch four holes around the rim of one cup. There should be a hole on each side. Push one straw across through two of the holes. Do the same with the other straw.

Poke a hole in the middle of the cup bottom. Push a pencil through, eraser first.

Push the pushpin through the straws where they cross. Then push it into the eraser.

Punch two holes in one side of the other cups. Slide each cup onto the end of a straw. The cups should face the same way.

Mark one cup with a big X.
Put clay around the pencil
bottom to make it stand up.

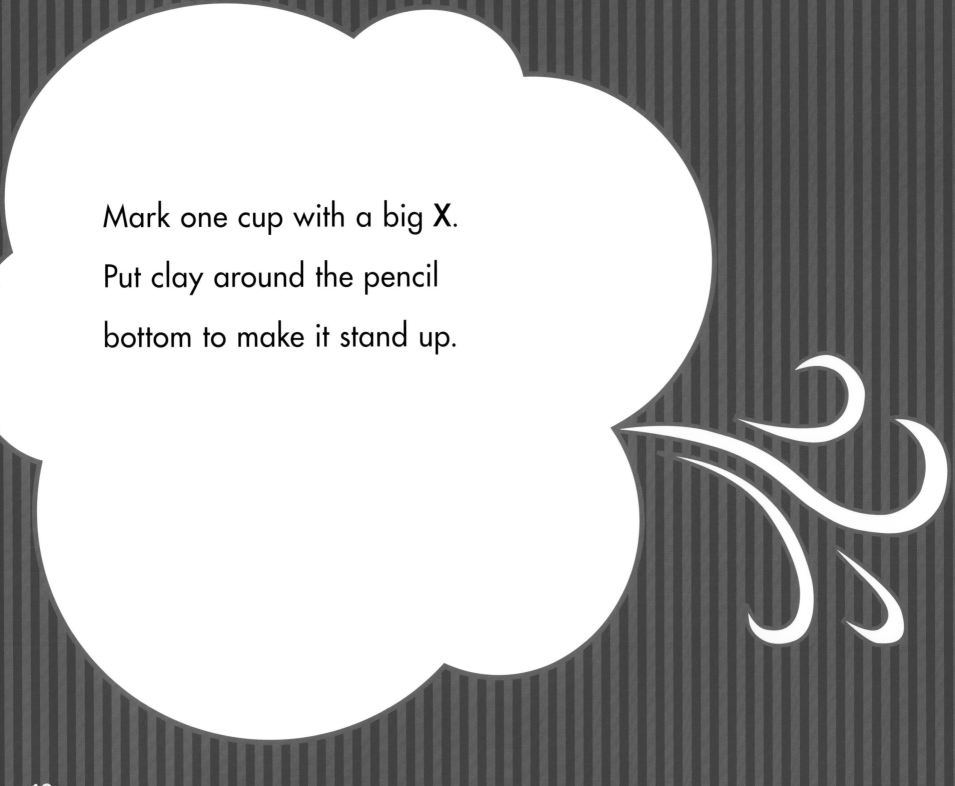

13

Put the meter in front of the fan. Start the fan on low. Set the timer for 20 seconds. Count how many times the X goes by in that time.

Write it down. Do this with the other fan speeds.

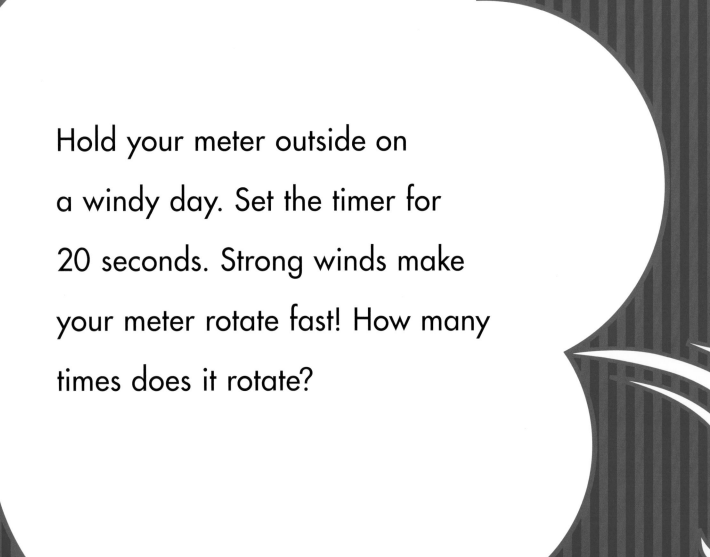

Hold your meter outside on a windy day. Set the timer for 20 seconds. Strong winds make your meter rotate fast! How many times does it rotate?

How Does It Work?

Your wind speed meter is called an anemometer. This tool measures wind speed. It helps scientists predict what weather is coming.

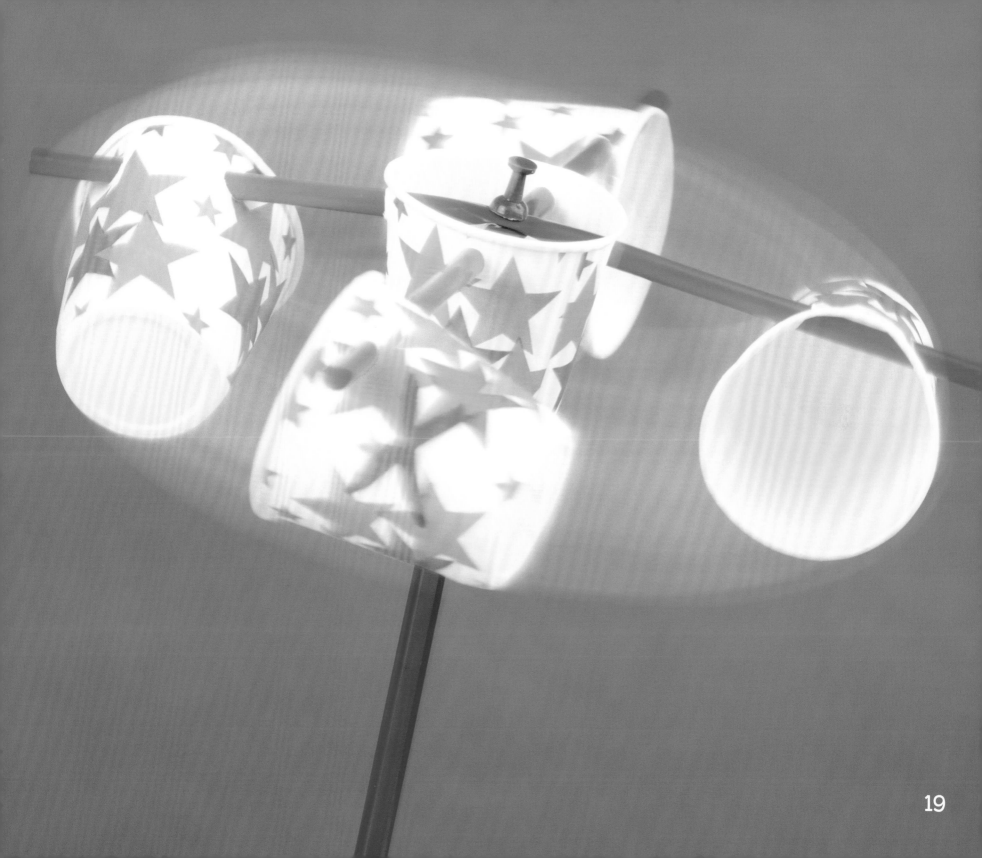

19

A change in wind speed can mean a weather change. Strong winds? A storm may be coming. Light winds? Plan a picnic!

Glossary

anemometer—a tool that measures wind speed

measure—to find out the speed, size, amount, weight, or strength of something

meter—a machine that counts or measures

pattern—something that repeats in the same way several times

predict—to say what you think will happen in the future

rotate—to move in a circle around a center point

Read More

De Seve, Karen. *Little Kids First Big Book of Weather.* Little Kids First Big Books. Washington, D.C.: National Geographic Kids, 2017.

Rustad, Martha E. H. *When Will It Rain?: Noticing Weather Patterns.* Nature's Patterns. Minneapolis: Millbrook Press, 2016.

Sohn, Emily. *Experiments in Earth Science and Weather With Toys and Everyday Stuff.* Fun Science. North Mankato, Minn.: Capstone Press, 2016.

Internet Sites

Use FactHound to find Internet sites related to this book.

Visit *www.facthound.com*

Just type 9781977102270 and go.

Super-cool stuff! Check out projects, games and lots more at
www.capstonekids.com

Critical Thinking Questions

1. What are some ways we can notice a change in wind speed without using an anemometer?

2. Why do you think the cups need to face the same way on your wind speed meter?

3. Can you think of a science tool that could measure wind direction? Why would it be important to know that?

Index